_____

To

_____

From

This book is dedicated to all those who serve,
have been served, and especially to The Servant
of all—Jesus Christ. May we be more like him
each day and embrace the awesome privilege we
have been given of serving him!

RON & CAESAR

THE HEART
OF A
Servant

BY RON DiCIANNI

COMPILED BY CAESAR KALINOWSKI

Tyndale House Publishers
WHEATON, ILLINOIS

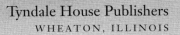

Visit Tyndale's exciting Web site at www.tyndale.com

For more information on this image or any of Ron's work, please call 800-391-1136 or visit us on-line at www.art2see.com

Designed by Melinda Schumacher

Scripture quotations marked KJV are taken from the *Holy Bible*, King James Version.

Scripture quotations marked NCV are taken from the *Holy Bible*, New Century Version, copyright © 1987, 1988, 1991 by Word Publishing, Dallas, Texas 75039. Used by permission.

Scripture quotations marked NIV are taken from the *Holy Bible*, New International Version ®. NIV ®. Copyright © 1973, 1978, 1984 by International Bible Society. Used by permission of Zondervan Publishing House. All rights reserved.

Scripture quotations marked NLT are taken from the *Holy Bible*, New Living Translation, copyright © 1996. Used by permission of Tyndale House Publishers, Inc., Wheaton, Illinois 60189. All rights reserved.

Scripture quotations marked TLB are taken from the *The Living Bible* copyright © 1971. Used by permission of Tyndale House Publishers, Inc., Wheaton, Illinois 60189. All rights reserved.

ISBN 0-8423-3420-3

Printed in Italy

07 06 05 04 03 02 01
7   6   5   4   3   2   1

SERVICE TO OTHERS

There is an art to serving others.
It is found in trusting God for your own needs,
which in turn will free you to look to the service of others.

Ron DiCianni

*Your attitude should be
the same that Christ Jesus had.*

*Though he was God,
he did not demand and cling to
his rights as God.*

*He made himself nothing;
he took the humble position of a slave and
appeared in human form.*

*And in human form
he obediently humbled himself even further
by dying a criminal's death on a cross.*

*Because of this,
God raised him up to the heights of heaven
and gave him a name
that is above every other name.*

—Philippians 2:5-9, nlt

*To serve is beautiful, but only
if it is done with joy and a whole
heart and a free mind.*

—PEARL S. BUCK

⌘

Blessed is the servant who esteems himself
no more highly when he is praised and exalted by people
than when he is considered worthless, foolish, and to be despised;
since what a man is before God, that he is and nothing more.

—FRANCIS OF ASSISI

There is no limit to what a man can do or where he can go
if he doesn't mind who gets the credit.

—SIGN ON RONALD REAGAN'S DESK

We find it encouraging to think of ourselves as God's servants. Who would not want to be a servant of the King? But when it comes to serving other people, we begin to question the consequences. We feel noble when serving God; we feel humble when serving people. Serving God receives a favorable response; serving people, especially those who cannot repay, has no visible benefit or glory from anyone—except from God! Christ gave us the example: "The Son of Man did not come to be served, but to serve, and to give His life as a ransom for many" (Matthew 20:28). To be a servant of God we must be a servant of people.

—CHARLES R. SWINDOLL
Improving Your Serve: The Art of Unselfish Living

※

For you have been called to live in freedom—not freedom to satisfy your sinful nature, but freedom to serve one another in love.

—GALATIANS 5:13, NLT

※

The purpose of human life is to serve and to show compassion and the will to help others.

—ALBERT SCHWEITZER

We can do no great things— only small things with great Love.

—MOTHER TERESA

He poured water into a basin and began
to wash his disciples' feet, drying them with
the towel that was wrapped around him.

He came to Simon Peter, who said to him,
"Lord, are you going to wash my feet?"

Jesus replied, "You do not realize now what
I am doing, but later you will understand."

"No," said Peter; "you shall never wash my feet."
Jesus answered, "Unless I wash
you, you have no part with me."

"Now that I, your Lord and Teacher,
have washed your feet, you also should wash
one another's feet.

I have set you an example that you should
do as I have done for you.

Now that you know these things, you will be
blessed if you do them."

—John 13:5-8, 14-15, 17, niv

The vocation of every man and woman is to serve other people.

—LEO TOLSTOY

❧

Jesus Christ was a workingman. His hands were fitted to labor as his voice was fitted to music. He entered into the condition of the great majority of mankind and became one of them in the fellowship of toil and from that time it has been hard for a man to get into better company than that of working people.

—GEORGE HALL

Carry each

$\mathcal{E}$verywhere Love Turns it finds burdens to carry and ways to help. Love is the teaching of Christ. To love means to wish another person good from the heart. It means to seek what is best for the other person. What if there were no one who made a mistake? What if no one fell? What if no one needed someone to help him? To whom would you show love? To whom could you show favor? Whose best could you seek? Love would not be able to exist if there were no people who made mistakes and sinned. The philosophers say that each of these people is the appropriate and adequate "object" of love or the "material" with which love has to work. The corrupt nature—or the kind of love that is really lust—wants others to wish it well and give it what it desires. In other words, it seeks its own interests. The "material" it works with is a righteous, holy, godly,

other's burdens

and good person. People who follow this corrupt nature completely reverse God's teaching. They want others to bear their burdens, serve them, and carry them. These are the kind of people who despise having uneducated, useless, angry, foolish, troublesome, and gloomy people as their life companions. Instead they look for friendly, charming, good-natured, quiet, and holy people. They don't want to live on earth but in paradise, not among sinners but among angels, not in the world but in heaven. We should feel sorry for these people because they are receiving their reward here on earth and possessing their heaven in this life.

—MARTIN LUTHER, *By Faith Alone*

*Share each other's troubles and problems, and
in this way obey the law of Christ.*

—Galatians 6:2, NLT

*He alone loves the Creator
perfectly who manifests a pure love
for his neighbor.*

—The Venerable Bede

*A cheerful giver does not count the cost
of what he gives.
His heart is set on pleasing and cheering
him to whom the gift is given.*

—Julian of Norwich

It is not great talents God blesses so much as
great likeness to the Lord Jesus.
A holy ministry is an awful weapon in the hands of God.

—ROBERT MURRAY McCHEYNE

*Unless we perform divine service
with every willing act of our life,
we never perform it at all.*

—JOHN RUSKIN

Well done, good and faithful servant!
You have been faithful with a few things;
I will put you in charge of many things.
Come and share your master's happiness!

—MATTHEW 25:23, NIV

Serve wholeheartedly,
as if you were serving the Lord,
not men.

—Ephesians 6:7, NIV

Do not turn your back on the needy, but share everything with your brother and call nothing your own. For if you have what is eternal in common, how much more should you have what is transient.

—The Didache

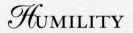

Humility

Truly humble people are unaware of their humility.
They are merely imitating Christ. And in this, he is their focus.

Ron DiCianni

*L*ord, my heart is not haughty, nor mine eyes lofty: neither do I exercise myself in great matters, or in things too high for me.

—Psalms 131:1, KJV

*W*ho are you trying to impress? Aim not for prestige, rather look for a place where you can serve. If God wants you to serve on a higher scale, he will invite you to a higher place.

—Dave Veerman/C.F.K.

More than any other single way,
the grace of humility is worked into our lives
through the discipline of service.

—Richard J. Foster, *Celebration of Discipline*

Humility is the foundation of all the other virtues;
hence, in the soul in which this virtue does not
exist there cannot be any other virtue except
in mere appearance.

—St. Augustine

Pride renders faith impossible.

—Andrew Murray, *Humility*

*Before destruction the heart of
man is haughty, and before honour
is humility.*

—Proverbs 18:12, KJV

❧

*The first step towards humility [is]
to realize that one is proud.*

—C. S. Lewis

❧

*Do not consider yourself to have
made any spiritual progress, unless you
account yourself the least of all men.*

—Thomas à Kempis

I never was truly happy until I ceased to wish to be great.

—Unknown

When we are totally emptied of ourselves, we can be full of the Holy Spirit. Then we are conquerors, and are able to accept all things from his hand. Besides this, we are being prepared to inherit all things.

—Corrie ten Boom

God does everything he does to exalt his mercy and abase man's pride.

The nature and depth of human pride are illuminated by comparing boasting to self-pity. Both are manifestations of pride. Boasting is the response of pride to success. Self-pity is the response of pride to suffering. Boasting says, "I deserve admiration because I have achieved so much." Self-pity says, "I deserve admiration because I have sacrificed so much." Boasting is the voice of pride in the heart of the strong. Self-pity is the voice of pride in the heart of the weak. Boasting sounds self-sufficient. Self-pity sounds self-sacrificing.

—JOHN PIPER, *Desiring God*

That in the coming ages he might
show the incomparable riches of his grace. . . .
For it is by grace you have been saved . . .
it is the gift of God . . . so that no one can boast.

—EPHESIANS 2:7-9, NIV

He predestined us to be adopted as his sons through
Jesus Christ . . . to the praise of his glorious grace.

—EPHESIANS 1:5-6, NIV

He chose the lowly things of this world
and the despised things . . .
so that no one may boast before him.

—1 CORINTHIANS 1:28-29, NIV

Be humble
and gentle.
Be patient
with each other,
making allowance for
each other's faults
because of
your love.

— Ephesians 4:2, nlt

You mortals, the Lord has told you what is good. This is what the Lord requires from you: to do what is right, to love mercy, and to live humbly with your God.

—Micah 6:8

* * *

Believers humble themselves by recognizing and looking at their weaknesses and sin. They try to avoid feeling proud of their works or of the gifts of the Spirit they have received from God. This is what it means "to live humbly with your God." We should be genuinely modest and humble, wanting to remain in the background. We should never look for honor and praise from the good works we do.

—Martin Luther
By Faith Alone

* * *

Why do you look at the speck of sawdust in your brother's eye and pay no attention to the plank in your own eye?

—Matthew 7:3, niv

* * *

Do nothing out of selfish ambition or vain conceit, but in humility consider others better than yourselves.

—Philippians 2:3, niv

Pride ends in a fall, while humility brings honor.

—Proverbs 29:23, TLB

Don't praise yourself; let others do it!

—Proverbs 27:2, TLB

Humility is a strange thing;
the moment you think you have it, you have lost it.

—Anonymous

Humility is to make a right estimate of one's self.

—Spurgeon

This is the deepest degree of humility:
to rejoice when one is humiliated and jeered at,
just as the vain person takes pride in great honors;
and to feel hurt when honored and esteemed,
as the proud person suffers when taunted and ridiculed.

—St. Francis de Sales

✦

Pride will push you to seek places you think you deserve
rather than where God has chosen you to serve.

—C. Gene Wilkes, *Jesus on Leadership*

✦

If you have any good things, believe better things of others,
that you may keep your meekness.

—Thomas à Kempis

The primary virtue of all, which is the love
of God and neighbor, originates in the light of humility.

—Angela of Foligno

The high and lofty one who inhabits eternity,
the Holy One, says this:
"I live in that high and holy place with those whose spirits
are contrite and humble. I refresh the humble and give new courage
to those with repentant hearts."

—Isaiah 57:15, NLT

Humility is the blossom of which death to self is the perfect fruit.

—Simone Weil

Pardon cannot precede repentance,
and repentance only begins with humility.

—Henri Amiel

Service to God

Service must be preceded by surrender.
Somewhere between salvation and maturity in Christ
our prayers should turn from "give me" to "use me."
Until then, we are quite useless to God.

Ron DiCianni

His lord said unto him,

"Well done, thou good and faithful servant:

thou hast been faithful

over a few things,

I will make thee ruler over many things:

enter thou into the joy of thy lord."

—Matthew 25:21, KJV

Blessed are they who keep [the Lord's] statutes and seek him with all their heart. They do nothing wrong; they walk in his ways.

—Psalm 119:2-3, NIV

No one gives himself freely and willingly to God's service unless, having tasted His fatherly love, he is drawn to love and worship Him in return.

—John Calvin

*W*e should serve God even if there is
darkness enveloping our

I will praise the Lord at all times;

life and even if we don't understand
what's happening . . .

his praise is always on my lips.

even when the circumstances of our life
don't make sense:

My whole being praises the Lord.

Because he is worthy of praise,
Because he is God.

—PSALM 34:1-2, NCV
MAX LUCADO, *Walking with the Savior*

Therefore I glory in Christ Jesus in my service to God.

—ROMANS 15:17, NIV

❧

Teach me, O Lord, Thy holy way, And give me an obedient mind; That in Thy service I may find My soul's delight from day to day.

—WILLIAM T. MATSON

Lord, you establish peace for us;
all that we have accomplished you
have done for us.

—ISAIAH 26:12, NIV

My Father and my God, grant in all
my service to You that I will be
hidden behind the cross, and the
voice that people hear will not be
mine alone, but the still small voice of
the Holy Spirit speaking to them. In
Christ's name I pray. Amen.

—SELWYN HUGHES, *Every Day Light*

*Teach us, Good Lord, to serve you
as you deserve.*

To give and not count the cost:

To fight and not to heed the wounds:

To toil and not to seek for rest:

To labor and not to ask for any reward

*Save that of knowing that
we do your will.*

—IGNATIUS OF LOYOLA

Firm and steadfast in good works
Make me, and in thy service
Make me to persevere.

—CLAIRE OF ASSISI

*O*Master, let me walk with Thee
In lowly paths of service free;
Tell me Thy secret; help me bear
The strain of toil, the fret of care.

—WASHINGTON GLADDEN

*O*Lord our God, refresh us with
quiet sleep, when we are wearied
with the day's labor; that being
assisted with the help which our
weakness needs, we may be devoted
to thee both in body and mind:
through Jesus Christ our Lord.

—LEONINE SACRAMENTARY

Remember
that the Lord
will give you
an inheritance
as your reward,
and the Master
you are serving
is Christ.

—COLOSSIANS 3:24, NLT

He must increase, but I must decrease.

—John 3:30, KJV

Oh! for a self-emptied spirit—a heart at leisure from itself—a mind delivered from all anxiety about one's own things! May we be more thoroughly delivered from self, in all its detestable windings and workings! Then could the Master use us, own us, and bless us.

—C. H. Mackintosh

*I will be faithful
. . . I will serve You.
Choose for yourselves this day
whom you will serve.*

—Joshua 24:15, NIV

Your choice must be a deliberate determination—it

is not something into which you will automatically

drift. And everything else in your life will be held in

temporary suspension until you make a decision.

The proposal is between you and God—do not

"confer with flesh and blood" about it.

—Oswald Chambers
   My Utmost for His Highest

*B*ut then something happened! For it pleased God in his kindness to choose me and call me, even before I was born! What undeserved mercy! Then he revealed his Son to me so that I could proclaim the Good News about Jesus to the Gentiles. When all this happened to me, I did not rush out to consult with anyone else.

—Galations 1:15-16, nlt

*W*here can any of us escape from his mighty hand? What world will receive anyone who deserts from his service?

—Clement of Rome

Servant Leadership

If you honestly love those you have been privileged to lead, you will want to be more of a servant to them than a boss. The greatest example of this was Christ, who washed feet with the same hands that created them.

Ron DiCianni

But Jesus called them together and said, "You know that in this world kings are tyrants, and officials lord it over the people beneath them.

But among you it should be quite different. Whoever wants to be a leader among you must be your servant, and whoever wants to be first must become your slave.

For even I, the Son of Man, came here not to be served but to serve others, and to give my life as a ransom for many."

—MATTHEW 20:25-28, NLT

*The high destiny
of the individual is to serve
rather than to rule.*

—ALBERT EINSTEIN

✳

"Shepherd is not a figure of strong over weak or
'lords' over servants. Quite the contrary. The
shepherd figure is one of love, service and openness.

Good spiritual leaders are shepherds, not saviours,
leaders not lords, guides not gods."

—LYNN ANDERSON, *They Smell Like Sheep*

But I am among you as one who serves.

Once we realize that Jesus has served us even to the depths of our meagerness, our selfishness, and our sin, nothing we encounter from others will be able to exhaust our determination to serve others for His sake.

—OSWALD CHAMBERS, *My Utmost for His Highest*

In Jesus the service of God and the service of the least of the brethren were one.

—DIETRICH BONHOEFFER

Whoever wants to save his life will lose it, but whoever loses his life for me will find it.

—MATTHEW 16:25, NIV

The spiritual authority of Jesus is an authority not found in a position or a title, but in a towel. As the cross is the sign of submission, so the towel is the sign of service.

—RICHARD J. FOSTER
Celebration of Discipline

True greatness, true leadership, is achieved not by reducing men to one's service but in giving oneself in selfless service to them.

—J. OSWALD SANDERS
Spiritual Leadership

Be sure to fear the Lord and serve him faithfully with all your heart; consider what great things he has done for you.

— 1 SAMUEL 12:24, NIV

You are a light in the darkness—a servant of God who is being watched, who gives off a very distinct message . . . often with hardly a word being said. At first they may hate the light—but don't worry, they are still attracted to it. Let it shine! Don't attempt to show off how bright or sparkling you are, just shine!

—CHARLES R. SWINDOLL
Improving Your Serve: The Art of Unselfish Living

If you are in a higher position or above others in some way, realize that God has given it to you. Don't make the mistake of bragging about it and lording it over others as if you were better than them in God's sight. Rather, God has commanded that you should humble yourself and use your position to serve your neighbor.

—MARTIN LUTHER, *By Faith Alone*

[*Jesus said,*] "I have set you an example that you should do as I have done for you. I tell you the truth, no servant is greater than his master, nor is a messenger greater than the one who sent him."

—JOHN 13:15-16, NIV

We who lead often overlook that the true place of Christ-like leadership is out in the crowd rather than up at the head table.

—C. GENE WILKES, *Jesus on Leadership*

Make a rule, and pray God to help you to keep it, never, if possible, to lie down at night without being able to say, "I have made one human being, at least, a little wiser, a little happier, or a little bit better this day."

—CHARLES KINGSLEY

You can make more friends in two months by becoming interested in other people than you can in two years by trying to get other people interested in you.

—DALE CARNEGIE

Leaders are stewards of God's purposes and resources in human lives. Too easily we act as if we were the owners. Too easily we try to play God. We do not work miracles for God. He does them for us.

—RICHARD KRIEGBAUM, *Leadership Prayers*

Do not be afraid!...
For the battle is not yours,
but God's.

—2 CHRONICLES 20:15, NLT